The Princess and the Frog

and the

Readers' Theater
How to Put on a Production

A Readers' Theater
Script and Guide

By Nancy K. Wallace • Illustrated by Michelle Henninger

magic wagon

visit us at www.abdopublishing.com

To my daughters, Mollie and Elizabeth, who have spent endless hours helping with library plays! —NKW

Published by Magic Wagon, a division of the ABDO Group, PO Box 398166, Minneapolis, Minnesota 55439. Copyright © 2014 by Abdo Consulting Group, Inc. International copyrights reserved in all countries. All rights reserved. No part of this book may be reproduced in any form without written permission from the publisher.

Looking Glass Library™ is a trademark and logo of Magic Wagon.

Printed in the United States of America, North Mankato, Minnesota.
052013
092013

 This book contains at least 10% recycled materials.

Written by Nancy K. Wallace
Illustrations by Michelle Henninger
Edited by Stephanie Hedlund and Rochelle Baltzer
Cover and interior design by Renée LaViolette

Library of Congress Cataloging-in-Publication Data
Wallace, Nancy K.
  The princess and the frog : a readers' theater script and guide / by Nancy K. Wallace ; illustrated by Michelle Henninger.
     pages cm. -- (Readers' theater: how to put on a production)
  Includes bibliographical references and index.
  ISBN 978-1-61641-989-9 (alk. paper)
1. Princesses--Juvenile drama. 2. Fairy tales--Adaptations--Juvenile drama. 3. Theater--Production and direction--Juvenile literature. 4. Readers' theater--Juvenile literature. I. Henninger, Michelle, illustrator. II. Title.
  PS3623.A4436P875 2013
  812'.6--dc23
                          2013011581

Table of Contents

School Plays

Do you like to act, make props, create weird sound effects, or paint scenery? You should put on a production. Plays are lots of fun! And a play is a great way for kids to work together as a team!

A readers' theater production can be done very simply. You just read your lines. You don't have to memorize them! An adapted readers' theater production looks more like a regular play. The performers wear makeup and costumes. The stage has scenery and props. The cast moves around to show the action. But, performers can still read their scripts.

To hold a production, you will need a large space. An auditorium with a stage is ideal. A classroom will work, too. Now, choose a date and get permission to use the space.

Finally, make flyers or posters to advertise your play. Place them around your school and community. Tell your friends and family. Everyone enjoys watching kids perform!

Cast & Crew

There are many people needed to put on a production. First, decide who will play each part. Each person in the cast will need a script. All the performers should practice their lines.

The Princess and the Frog has a lot of speaking parts.

Narrator - The storyteller

Frederick - An enchanted frog

Princess Lily - The only daughter of the king

Frog #1 - The director of the frog chorus

Frog #2 - A member of the frog chorus

Frog Chorus - At least three frogs but you can have as many as you like!

Next, a crew is needed. The show can't go on without these important people! Some jobs can be combined. Every show needs a director. This person organizes everything and everyone in the show.

The director works with the production crew. This includes the costume designers, who borrow or make all the costumes. Stage managers make sure things run smoothly.

Your production can also have a stage crew. This includes lighting designers to run spotlights and other lighting. Set designers plan and make scenery. The special effects crew takes care of sound and other unusual effects.

Sets & Props

At a readers' theater production, the performers sit on stools at the front of the room. But, an adapted readers' theater production or full play will require some sets and props.

Sets include a background for each scene of the play. Props are things you'll need during the play. *The Princess and the Frog* could have the following set and props:

Scene Set - The entire play takes place in a castle garden. Cut the top, bottom, and one side out of a large cardboard box to make a wishing well. You will have one long piece of cardboard with two folds in it. Paint the outside of the cardboard to look like stones. Set it up on stage so that the front of the box faces the audience. Angle the two sides to allow a large opening in the back for Frederick to get in and out of the well. Add real or fake flowers in pots to look like a garden.

Props - Frog #1 needs a music stand and a stick to use as his baton. Paint large circles of cardboard to look like the sun and the moon. Glue them to paint sticks. Princess Lily's ball should be sparkly and pretty. Make huge pink lips out of cardboard and glue them to a paint stick for the kiss. Make a glittery sign out of cardboard that says "POOF!" It should be large enough to cover Frederick when he is on his knees.

You'll also need tickets that list important information. Be sure to include the title of the play and where it will take place. List the date and time of your performance.

Your production can also have a playbill. It is a printed program. The front of a playbill has the title of the play, the date, and the time. Playbills list all of the cast and production team inside.

Makeup & Costumes

The stage and props aren't the only things people will be looking at in your play! The makeup artist has a big job. Stage makeup needs to be brighter than regular makeup. Even boys wear stage makeup!

Costume designers set the scene just as much as set designers. They borrow costumes or adapt old clothing for each character. For example, you can make a cloak out of a length of fabric gathered at the neck. Ask adults if you need help finding or sewing costumes.

The Princess and the Frog performers will need these costumes:

Narrator - A shirt and pants with a cloak

Frederick - A green top and pants and large plastic glasses. Some online sources also have inexpensive frog hats.

Frederick as the dog - Change top to brown or black. Add a headband with dog ears out of felt or fake fur.

Princess Lily - A fancy dress

Frog #1 - A green top and pants with a frog hat

Frog #2 - A green top and pants with a frog hat

Frog Chorus - A green top and pants with a frog hat

Stage Directions

When your sets, props, and costumes are ready, it is important to rehearse. Choose a time that everyone can attend. Try to have at least five or six rehearsals before your show.

You should practice together as a team, even if you will be reading your scripts for readers' theater. A play should sound like a conversation. Try to avoid pauses when no one is speaking. You can do this by adding sound effects.

Some theater terms may seem strange. The **wings** are the sides of the stage that the audience can't see. The **house** is where the audience sits. The **curtains** refers to the main curtain at the front of the stage.

When reading your script, the stage directions are in parentheses. They are given from the performer's point of view. You will be facing the audience when you are performing. Left will be on your left and right will be on your right. When rehearsing, perform the stage directions and the lines to get used to moving around the stage.

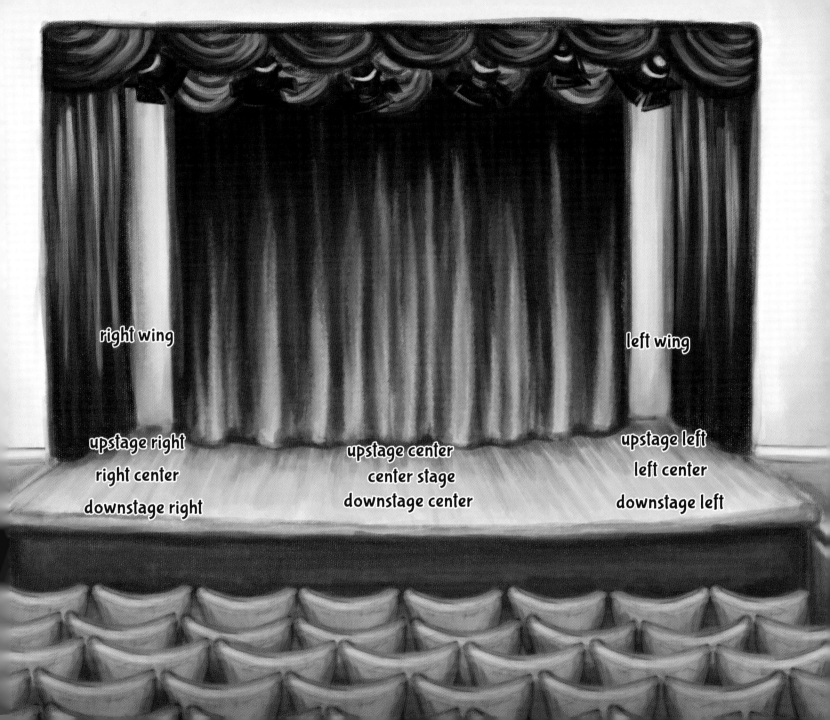

Script: *The Princess and the Frog*

(Opening Curtain: Narrator sits at stage right. The wishing well is at center stage with a music stand in front of it. The Frog Chorus hops on and kneels at downstage center.)

Narrator: Scene 1— The Castle Garden. Once upon a time, a very long time ago, there was a princess.

Frederick: *(Enters stage left)* What about me?

Narrator: I'll get to your part in a minute. As I was saying, once upon a time there was a princess—a very beautiful princess, in fact.

Frederick: And a very handsome frog.

Narrator: *(Turning to look at him)* Actually, you are a very clever frog. And, if you remember, there are quite a few other frogs in this story.

Frederick: I'm the only important one.

Frog Chorus: *(Angrily)* Hey!

Narrator: That's your opinion. All frogs are important!

Frog Chorus: *(Put right fists in the air)* Yes!

Narrator: Now, all of you important frogs need to sit quietly while I tell this story. *(Pointing at Frederick)* You sit over there! And the rest of you sit over there!

(All frogs sigh very loudly. The Frog Chorus sits down in a semi-circle around the well facing the audience. Frederick stands to one side.)

Frederick: *(Tapping his foot loudly)* It's very hard to wait.

Narrator: *(Ignoring him)* Now, the king of the land was a very powerful man. His daughter, Lily, had everything she could ever wish for.

Frederick: *(Throwing his hands out dramatically)* Except for a frog.

(Princess walks in from stage left. A member of the stage crew follows her with the sun.)

Narrator: One afternoon, Princess Lily was walking in the garden.

Frederick: *(Holding up a finger)* Wait a minute! It was evening and she was playing with her ball.

Narrator: *(Angrily)* Would you like to tell the story?

Frederick: I'd love to! I've never understood why stories need a narrator anyway. Why don't you just sit over there! *(Pointing)*

Narrator: *(Sits on the edge of the stage)* Whatever!

(Princess and the stage crew with the sun exit the stage looking annoyed. Curtains close.)

Narrator: Scene 2 — The Castle Garden

(Curtains open. Frederick is wearing the narrator's cloak. The princess enters from stage left followed by a stage crew member with the moon.)

Frederick: Once upon a time there was a beautiful princess. One evening, she was playing with her ball in the castle garden. It was almost dark and the full moon shone brightly. She could hear the frogs singing by the wishing well. *(Points to Frog Chorus)* Okay guys, you're on!

Frog Chorus: *(The Chorus is divided into three sections. The first says* peep, peep. *The second says* croak, croak. *The third says* chirr-ump, chirr-ump. *Each part follows the first with no pause in between. As each section sings, the frogs in that section should stand up and then sit down immediately. Frog #1 is the director. He taps a stick against his music stand, clears his throat and then holds the stick up as a signal for the Frog Chorus to begin.)* Peep, peep, croak, croak, chirr-ump, chirr-ump. *(Repeat three times.)*

Frederick: Just then a handsome frog entered the garden. *(Frederick whips off his cloak and throws it to the narrator)* Ribbit, ribbit!

Frog #1: *(Holds up his hand for the others to stop singing)* Whoa, you're not from around here, are you?

Frederick: *(Swaggering toward them)* No, I'm not. In fact, my name is Sir Frederick!

(The Frog Chorus gasps.)

Frog #2: But, you look like a frog!

Frederick: Looks can be deceiving. What if I told you that I've been enchanted by an evil sorceress?

(The Frog Chorus gasps again and backs away.)

Frederick: Don't worry! She lives far away in another kingdom. I doubt she will ever visit your little garden. But someday I will live in a castle again and eat every meal with a beautiful princess.

Frog #1: I'm really sorry. I had no idea who you were. You look like an ordinary, little, green frog. Is there anything we can do to help you?

Frederick: I'm afraid you can't help me. *(He points to the princess)* But, Princess Lily can. I just have to convince her to kiss me.

Frog #1: *(Looks disgusted)* She's not going to kiss you!

Frederick: Yes, she will. Sing your song again. Maybe she'll come a little closer.

Frog #2: I really liked that song you were singing.

Frederick: That's what all the frogs sing in my kingdom. Repeat after me. Ribbit, ribbit!

Frog Chorus: Peep, peep, croak, croak, chirr-ump, chirr-ump. *(Then all say together)* Ribbit, ribbit! *(Repeat three times.)*

Princess Lily: (Moving nearer) That's odd. The frogs sound different tonight!

Frog Chorus: Peep, peep, croak, croak, chirr-ump, chirr-ump, ribbit, ribbit! (Repeat three times)

Princess: I wonder what's wrong with them.

(Frog Chorus should continue to sing quietly in the background.)

Princess: (Throws her ball in the air and catches it) Oh dear, I wish I had someone to play with. It's not much fun playing ball alone.

Frederick: Here is my chance to speak to the princess!

Frog #1: *(Rushing over and whispering)* Stop, Sir Frederick! Frogs aren't supposed to speak to princesses!

Frederick: Why not?

Frog #2: Because we are *frogs.*

Frederick: I've never heard of anything so silly! Everyone should be allowed to speak to everyone else. Anyway, I'm not really a frog. *(Bowing deeply and then sitting down)* Your majesty, allow me to introduce myself. I am Sir Frederick and I would love to play ball with you.

Princess: *(Looking around)* Who said that?

Frederick: Me, I'm down here by your feet.

Princess: Ewww! You're nothing but a nasty, little, green frog. I was hoping for a handsome prince.

Frederick: Then it's your lucky day! I'm not really a frog. An evil sorceress cast a spell on me!

Princess: *(Hands on hips)* That only happens in fairy tales! I don't believe you.

Frederick: Oh well, it was worth a try. Can we still play ball, please?

Princess: Never mind, I'm not interested in playing with a frog. I'll just throw the ball myself. *(Waving her hand)* Why don't you hop off somewhere?

Frederick: *(Bowing)* As you wish.

Princess: *(Throws ball into the well)* Oh no! My ball went into the well. *(Looking down)* I can't even see it. The water is too deep. That was my favorite ball. *(She begins to cry and then looks up)* Frog? Where are you?

Frederick: Please call me *Sir Frederick*. Can I be of service?

Princess: I lost my ball in the well. Could you swim down and get it for me?

Frederick: Of course, I can. But why would I want to? You haven't been very nice to me.

Princess: I'm sorry. I have never talked to a frog before.

Frederick: Well, frogs have feelings too, just like everyone else. You think you are special just because you are a princess.

Princess: I apologized. What more do you want?

Frederick: (*Rubbing chin*) Let me see, maybe you could give me some kind of reward.

Princess: (*Sighing loudly*) I suppose you want a kiss? Ewww!

Frederick: Oh no. I was thinking more of a condo or a sports car.

Princess: *What?!* Just for getting my ball out of the well? You have *got* to be kidding!

Frederick: Perhaps you could just let me live in the castle with you. I could eat at your table and sleep in your room.

Princess: You ask too much.

Frederick: Well, then how about a kiss? I'll settle for that.

Princess: Well . . .

Frederick: (*Looking down into the well*) That water is very deep. You'll never see that ball again without my help.

Princess: Oh all right, you nasty thing! Find my ball and I'll give you a kiss!

Frederick: At your service! I'll only be a moment! (*Frederick enters well from behind and ducks down below the cardboard*)

Narrator: Scene 3 — The Castle Garden just a few minutes later . . .

Princess: *(Looking down into the well)* That frog has been gone a long time. What if he can't find it?

Narrator: *(Stepping forward)* Don't worry, he will.

Princess: How do you know?

Narrator: I'm the narrator. I know the whole story.

Frederick: *(Appearing with the ball)* Whew! Your ball was a long way down!

Princess: Ewww! It's all wet and muddy!

Frederick: So am I! Pucker up!

Princess: *(Backing away)* Wait! Wait! Wait! Let me think. Isn't there something else that you want?

Frederick: Sure! I'd settle for a really nice condo on the fifteenth floor with a view of the river. Or, I'd love a little red sports car with real leather seats!

Princess: You are ridiculous! Do you still want to live with me at the castle?

Frederick: *(Hopping up and down happily)* Yes! Yes! Can I eat at your table and sleep in your room?

Princess: For how long?

Frederick: For the rest of my life!

Narrator: I wonder how long *that* will be.

Princess: *(Disgusted)* I can't do that!

Frederick: Then you'll have to kiss me.

Princess: (*Sighs*) Oh, all right.

(*Frederick hops up closer to her.*)

Princess: Wait! Narrator, I have to know . . . is this frog really a handsome prince in disguise?

Narrator: Not exactly, but he isn't a frog either.

Princess: (*Sighs*) Some people have the worst luck! Come here, Frederick! (*Princess kisses Frederick using huge pink lips on a paint stick*)

(*Stage crew covers Frederick with a big cardboard sign that says POOF! Frederick the dog takes his place.*)

Narrator: Scene 4 – The Castle Garden a few minutes later . . .

Frederick: Bark! Bark!

Princess: You aren't a prince. You're a dog! *(Frederick takes the ball from her hand and runs on his hands and knees across the stage toward Frog #1)*

Frog #1: Wow, Frederick! Why didn't you tell us?

Frederick: I told you I was under a spell from an evil sorceress. I belonged to a princess in another kingdom, but now I'll never get back home. It took a kiss from another princess to turn back into a dog again.

Princess: (Clapping happily) I can't believe you're a dog! I've always wanted a dog! We can play ball in the garden, and you can live in the castle and sleep in my room! I'm so excited!

Narrator: And the princess and the frog—I mean dog—lived happily ever after.

Frog Chorus: Peep, peep, croak, croak, chirr-ump, chirr-ump, ribbit, ribbit! (Say only once.)

The End

Adapting Readers' Theater Scripts

Readers' theater can be done very simply. You just read your lines. You don't have to memorize them! Performers sit on chairs or stools. They will read their parts without moving around.

Adapted Readers' Theater

This looks more like a regular play. The performers wear makeup and costumes. The stage has scenery and props. The cast moves around to show the action. Performers can still read their scripts.

Hold a Puppet Show

Some schools and libraries have puppet collections. Students make the puppets be the actors. Performers can read their scripts.

Teacher's Guides

Readers' Theater Teacher's Guides are available online! Each guide includes reading levels for each character and additional production tips for each play. Visit Teacher's Guides at **www.abdopublishing.com** to get yours today!